The Writers Guidebook to Writing Love, Romance, and Sex Scenes

S L Lethe

Table of Contents

Introduction

Romance is the biggest selling category of fiction books on Amazon and there has been an increase of romance writers in recent years. Romance books have the ability to sweep you off your feet with a few words, with the incredible settings, and the heart-wrenching dialogue. New sub-categories of romance books have recently emerged, including clean, wholesome, romantic erotica, paranormal/fantasy romance, medical romance, billionaire, interracial, and many others.

Writing romance can be lots of fun, but it can get stressful when trying not to repeat the same old expression, sentence, or gesture over and over again. Conveying how your characters feel and what they experience is a great way of connecting with the reader, not just the characters, but you as the author as well. Readers are turned off by laze writing, and once you repeat the same line twice, you start becoming a lazy writer. You want to leave your readers breathless and aching to turn over the page.

As an author of romance books (including paranormal and interracial), it can be a little hard (no pun intended) to get the right words on the screen. Getting the images from your head into written form can be challenging and I did struggle with my gestures and body language in my early days. Today, it's much easier, especially since I write down notes and sentences that I can use for later books.

This book, as well as my others, have come about in order to keep my notes in order. I created lists of words, of descriptions, sounds, and gestures to help me. Recently, several authors have requested my notebooks so they, too, can reference them.

The Writer's Guidebook to Writing Love, Romance, and Sex Scenes is a list-based guide divided into several categories, making it easy and simply to reference when needed. There are hundreds of examples of sentences which deal with body gestures and language for non-sexual scenes (but does include kissing), body gestures and language for sexual scenes, emotions (both positive and negative), talking, facial descriptions, sounds, romantic settings, words used in sex scenes, and words used for genitalia.

These words and descriptions can be used or modified for your novels but will depend on your category and sub-genre. I have separated the sexual and non-sexual body gestures and language for those who write clean romance (meaning no sexual scenes). I have not included any specific LGBTQ content in this book, but you can easily gender-swap the descriptions. Since this book contains descriptions of a sexual nature, it is only intended for mature audiences.

Some of the descriptions will be better suited for particular romance categories, and many can be mixed with others to create a more thrilling sentence. Use them to create the ideal line for your character.

Happy writing!

Body Gestures and Language (Non-Erotic)

- He pulled her closer by the waist so fast that she couldn't even shake herself free
- She found her fingers laced together as she listened to his words
- She craned her neck and looked at him
- He pulled her into him
- He brushed a thumb over the soft pillow of her bottom lip
- Her lips fell open a fraction
- He urged her lips apart and swept into her mouth, shifting the kiss from persuasive to demanding
- He held her by the shoulder
- He cups a hand behind his ear
- He pulled her chin up so she could meet his eyes
- She pushed him away gently and held him by the arms
- She rolled her head and began to walk away
- He shook his head, wrinkling his nose
- She rested her cheek on her hand and sighed
- His lips curled, but he didn't release her hand
- She flushed as he busied herself behind the bar
- She stepped forward, extending a hand
- She grabbed a handful of his silk shirt and pulled him down to her
- He stayed on the balls of his feet, knees on either side of her body
- He lowered his head and brushed kisses across her jaw, her neck
- He was all she could see in the shop/office, the rest was nothing but a meaningless backdrop
- She looked over her, cocking her head as she appraised the smaller woman appreciatively
- Her eyes met his, a hint of competitive challenge in them before she turned back to [insert character]
- She reached out to touch the lock of hair on his forehead
- Despite her obvious confidence and sexual charm, she looked a little lost
- She went to her knees and kissed him
- She didn't turn around and face him
- She closed her eyes and inhaled all the air she could
- She turned around and smiled at his persistence
- She rose up on her tiptoes to kiss him on his grizzled cheek
- All she wanted was to be close enough for his musky scent to make her head swim with a heady intoxication
- There's no more hiding from his grin
- Their fingers entwined in a loose grip
- He leaned back and smiled
- He locked his mouth to hers like he would breathe her into himself

- Her fingers tangled in his hair, curling around the strands at his scalp, then using her grip to position him as she slanted her mouth across his own
- She nodded twice, saying nothing, looking at her feet
- She couldn't help but turn around and face him
- His long hands cupped her face, and then slid behind her head in the warmth of her hair
- He turned and dared her eyes
- He signalled for her to follow him
- With the nail of her thumb in her mouth she scanned the square, biting down harder than she had intended and swallowing the fragment.
- He began to run his lips down her neck
- There was a burning sensation of anticipation in her chest
- She moved with a sinuous grace that would have been at home on a dancer
- He ran his hand over her back, softly trailing it over her muscles
- She let out a laugh, releasing some of the tension
- She grabbed a handful of the t-shirt, balled it into both her fists, and pulled him those last few inches into a kiss
- Watching her carefully from the corner of his eyes
- Her movements were exquisitely languid, serpentine, and seductive
- His biceps were ringed with various tattooed designs
- He opened his mouth to argue, but her fingertips touched his lips and the protest died away
- He turned and walked away without waiting for her answer/reaction
- He paused and licked his lips
- He remained still, devouring her with his eyes
- She tried to press her body forward against his, but his hands held her back
- His lips pressed against hers like heat
- Straightening to his full height
- He sat comfortably in the armchair, exuding calmness and authority
- Throwing her hands up in surrender
- She shuddered in his hands from the feel of his mouth
- When their lips were only a whisper apart, she could feel her whole body begin to tremble
- He continued to hold onto her arm, but he loosened his grip with tenderness
- He moved a step closer to her, then another, the sound of his footsteps cutting through the silence of the room
- She kept her head turned because she knew she was blushing
- He held the sheet with his right hand
- He never stopped kissing her as his fingertips slid down her bare shoulders
- The sheet slipped down in front
- He caressed her shoulder, down her arm, until her fingers tangled with his
- She lifted her hips in blatant invitation
- His every muscle tensed
- She folded one leg over the other, dangling her high heel, showing more leg
- He pressed his stiff cock at the entrance of her swollen sex
- He stirred his drink with a long finger
- He drummed his fingers on the railing
- Seeking her hand with his own, he tangled their fingers together
- With his hand, he captured the back of her head and deepened their kiss

- Ignoring her quickening heartbeat, she stood to her full height, kept a poker face and tried to look him straight in the eye
- He kissed his way down her body, to her thigh
- His hands were insistent as he forced her chin upwards, so he was the only thing reflected in her eyes
- She slung a leg over his thighs and climbed on top of him, wriggling and pushing until she managed to take half on him
- Pinning her to the wall
- He swallowed the drink slowly, savouring the slow burn
- He curled one hand around her neck, the other anchored on her hip
- She tried to impale herself on his thick staff,
- They remained silent as they held each other's gaze
- The flavour of his kiss was still alive on her tongue
- She could feel her body ease up, letting go of the tension from her nervousness and surprise
- Her back suddenly met with the wall
- He reeked of sophistication and charm
- She wiggled her hips until he could go no further
- He dragged his lips across her soft skin and nibbled at her hipbone
- He dragged a thumb over the nub between her legs once more
- Her breath hitched, her back arched
- There was magic in his lips
- He pressed her closer to him as his body burned out of control
- She looked away from him, but his hand caught her chin and forced her to look back
- He ran his fingers down her bare arm in a tickling brush
- He stroked the curve of her face
- He helped her to her feet, laughing devilishly
- Leather-bound fingers grazed the bottom of her chin, tilting her head up
- His hands cupped her face, forcing her to finally look at him
- His hands ran through her hair, gently brushing the loose strands from her face
- His chest pressed against hers, smooth, warm
- With fevered kisses, he took her mouth with unrelenting passion
- Goosebumps perforated down her nape
- He stroked a finger down her cheek
- Bundling her fists into the fabric of his shirt
- A drop of water teased the curve of his lips
- His black top clung to the heard lines and dips of his torso in immaculate detail
- His top traced the path of his abs that her tongue wanted to follow desperately
- His thumb skimmed to the corner of her bottom lip then traced the seam
- He moved so that his body was pressed against hers
- With one fluid motion
- Pulling her flush to his body
- His fingers closed on her chin and began to turn her face slowly towards his
- His mouth hovered an inch above hers
- His arms tightened around her an instant before he lowered his lips to hers
- She took his groan into her mouth, savouring it, savouring him
- She crossed her arms over her ample bosom and leaned against the doorframe

- She looked up at him, her breath catching in her throat
- She tucked a wayward strand of hair behind her ear
- Her body sank into the feel of his arms wrapping around her
- He tasted like sin and paradise all rolled into one
- His hands closed around her waist
- His lips fluttered across her cheek, down her jaw, to her neck
- As he took her mouth in a hot and demanding kiss
- The muscles in his shoulders were tight as a violin's string
- Warm fingers brushed over her face
- Her breaths came in short bursts
- He touched her delicately, like a rose petal he didn't want to bruise
- He held her close enough that she could feel his breath on her ear
- His breath caressed her ear
- In a swirl of motion
- She placed a trembling hand against the width of his hot chest
- She paused and chewed her lip, lost in thought
- Beneath her hands, he flexed with tension
- He leaned toward her, his lips closing in
- She fidgeted with the hem of her shirt
- His shirt clung to him in all the right places
- Her hot breath fanned against his lips
- She took a tentative step back
- He stepped towards her and brushed a wayward strand of hair from her face
- She sank down on the edge of the bed
- Her arm extended as he brought her palm to his lips, lingering longer than what was necessary
- His hands slid from her curls, caressing down her arms, encircling her waist, until he grasped her hips
- Breath ragged and shallow, she clawed to get closer
- He took a deep breath before letting it out again
- A warm breeze picked up tendrils of her hair
- He placed a hand over his heart as if her words had wounded him
- He wagged his eyebrows at her
- His fingers slid over her knuckles and his thumb brushed against the inside of her palm
- In an instant, he moved toward her and wrapped his arms around her body, pulling her close
- Warm fingers closed around her chin
- He held out his arm for her
- She let him wrap his arms around her and kiss her
- She fidgeted, adjusting the strap of her dress and applying another coat to her already red lips
- She tucked her hand into the crook of his elbow
- Slowly, he reached out to touch her and paused, inches from her face
- He took her hand in his and studied their entwined fingers
- She laid the palm of her hand against the dark bristle on his cheek
- His hand cupped the crown of her head, fingers tangling in her hair
- He motioned her towards the passenger's seat and unlocked the car

- His fingers tensed in her hair
- Carefully, she circled the moist tip as his breathing turned ragged
- He moved slowly in her hand
- His breath rasped hot on her neck as he rained kisses there
- She worked her lips across his stubbled jaw
- Her fingertips hesitated, hovering just over the surface of his chest/face
- She melted into his arms, honey over fire
- Fingers curled around her hand
- As he brushed his knuckles down the side of her face
- He steadied her and pulled her closer in the process
- His fingers laced through her hair
- His breath stirred her hair
- He turned to glance back at her, his eyes heated and a cocky smile on his lips
- Before she could get any words out, he covered her mouth with his and kissed her
- He ran his fingers through his slightly unruly mane
- He paused, backing away enough to stare into her eyes
- He seized her lips in the next heartbeat
- He covered her mouth again, deepening his possession
- He leaned against the brick wall and crossed his arms
- She turned to look at him, sweeping her long hair out of her face
- The task took all his concentration to accomplish
- He shuddered in her arms as she explored the length of his shaft
- With an alluring curl of her fingers, she summoned him
- She latched slender arms around his neck and arched, distracting him with her lush curves
- He reared back in surprise, speculation on his face
- Groaning, he buried his face in her neck
- He stepped inside and shut the door behind him
- She covered her lush lips with her hand and stared at him as if the sight shocked her
- Her hand dropped from her mouth, and she bit her bottom lip
- He clamped large, heated fingers around her hips
- His fingers tightened, and he brought her closer
- He pulled back with a tender smile
- She raised a shaking hand to his chest to ward him off
- He stepped forward and wrapped his fingers around her elbow
- Clutching his shoulders
- There she sat, relearning how to breathe
- He brushed his hand down her spine to the small of her back
- She filtered her hands through the silky strands of his dark hair that hung to his shoulders
- He took her hand and brought it to his lips
- She smoothed a hand over the sleek bulge of his shoulder
- He fisted his hand deeper in her hair, pulling her even closer
- She reciprocated his handshake, but never would he trust a man so perfect, as far as he was concerned the more perfect the image the greater the danger underneath
- Her fingers traced along the hard edges of his jawline
- The sensitive surface of his mouth
- He slanted his mouth over hers once more, this possession his deepest yet

- Her hands climbed from his biceps to curl around his neck
- Tyler took his hands out of his pockets, suddenly unsure of where to put them
- She clutched at his shirt, dragging him against her
- She put her hands on his chest and rose on tiptoe to offer him her lips
- He moulded his body against hers, arms wrapping her arms against her chest
- He held her with his body and his arms, pressing so close she could feel his heart beating against her back/chest
- He draped an arm over her in an affectionate embrace
- He praised her with kisses across her jaw, down her neck
- She ran her hands over her arms as if to warm herself
- He captured her mouth in a slow kiss saturated with his longing to reach her heart
- He dusted light/fresh kisses onto the corners of her lips
- His hands slid over her waist
- He held out a hand, which she accepted with a shy/small nod
- He ran his fingers across her hand on the table
- She smiled, eyebrows raised and extended a manicured hand  — Describe
- He gently extracted himself from her grip
- She rubbed a soft thumb across his knuckles
- She wrapped her arms around his neck and tucked her head under his chin
- She tightened her hold on his neck
- Her breath tickled his neck
- She lifted her head to look at him
- He gently pulled her close even though he wanted to crush her against him
- He dipped his head and hovered his lips just over hers
- Her kiss was featherlight and sweet
- He buried his hand in her soft hair before he kissed her forehead
- She rocked on her heels, peering into the crowd
- He brushed her hair back from her neck before he leaned down to inhale deeply against her skin
- He looked up to lock gazes with her in the mirror
- She took his hand into hers and led it to her lips so that she could kiss the hard callouses there
- He dipped his head down to taste her lips one more time
- Reaching up, she cupped his face in her hands
- She brushed the hair back from his face an instant before she kissed him
- He pulled back to give her a look so tender that it brought an ache to her chest
- Without a word, he held out his hand to her
- She felt her jaw go slack at his news
- He moved to stand just behind her so that he could whisper into her ear
- His lips were scalding as they claimed hers
- She melted from the heat of that kiss
- She reached up to smooth the frown from his brow
- He released her so quickly that she was barely able to balance herself
- He moved to step around her so that her back was against his chest/front
- He leaned forward and inhaled that special scent of her hair
- She lifted his hand and held it between hers

Don't Be VAGUE

- He laid his hand against the smoothness of her cheek
- She lifted herself up on her toes until their gazes were almost level

Body Gestures – Sex Scenes

- She slowly fingered him from hilt to tip
- She watched as he spread her thighs wide an instant before he leaned down to take her into his mouth
- He pressed her hand against his swollen shaft
- She saw the pleasure on his face as she gently wrapped her hand around him
- He couldn't breathe at the tightness of her body welcoming his
- He spread her thighs wide before he sank himself into her again, going even deeper than he had before
- She couldn't breathe as she felt the hard thickness of him inside her again
- He arched his back, driving himself deep inside her
- He felt his breath rush out of him as she slowly took him into her mouth, inch by sweet inch
- His hands spilled over her breasts, cupping them, kneading them
- He slid up hands upwards slowly, so slowly that she wanted to cry out
- She lay with one hand entwined in his dark hair while his head was buried deep within her spread legs
- He watched as her nipples hardened under the fabric of her tunic, teasing his desire
- He cupped her breast as he pulled her back against him
- She tensed as he swiped his tongue over the needy bud again
- She cried out his name as she convulsed in climax
- She clung tight, then writhed against his erection
- He pressed inside her, gliding slowly over the spot that made her gasp
- He withdrew inch by torturous inch
- He held her to the mattress for slow thrusts and drugging kisses
- His tongue flicked across her nipple, fast, wet, quick
- She hissed at the sensation of his long, deep stroke
- Taking his cue, she rode him slowly, deeply
- Wanting more, he lifted his hips, driving himself even deeper into her body
- The water pooled around her breasts, the peaks jutting up
- He peppered the sensitive skin of her inner thighs with kisses
- She arched to meet his next thrust
- His hands went to his jeans, unsnapping them
- She nipped and tugged at his mouth with a boldness that surprised him
- He kissed her deeply as his hands explored her body
- He slowly kissed his way from her lips to her breast
- The sight of her bare, soft body had him unbearably hard
- He released her breast in one long pull so that the nipple stretched between his teeth
- He tasted of sin, smelled of pleasure
- Unable to stand it, he leaned down to capture one in his mouth
- He teased the soft nipple with his tongue as he moved in and out of her body
- He bit gently around the soft tissue of her breast, then licked the nipple, rolling it with his tongue
- A hot searing bolt of pleasure struck through her

- He sank his finger deep inside her
- She arched, moaning, as if every touch felt amazing
- Wildly, he pumped into her, revealing in the sensations
- As he cupped her breast, her sweet scent intoxicated him
- She buried her hand in his hair an instant before her cries of ecstasy filled his ears
- He watched the pleasure play across her face as he continued to ride her
- Burying himself deep, he shivered as his body burst into a thousand spasms
- The swollen folds of her flesh were a temptation he couldn't resist
- He gave one long, luscious lick to her that caused her to shudder
- She felt the tip of him hard and stern against her core
- His gaze held her captive as he slowly slid her onto his cock
- Once he was buried to his hilt, he held her there motionless
- Their bodies brushed, his heat crashing into her
- Biting her lip, she parted her thighs even more
- He towered over her, his cock nudging her belly
- She cried out as he slowly tongued her swollen nipple
- He gently sank his hand down her cleft
- She was suddenly naked, with him kneeling in front of her, staring up
- He put his hands on the insides of her thighs and spread her legs
- In that instant, his cock hardened
- His tongue raked her sex with one smooth, slick glide
- He dropped his hands to her thighs and pried them wider
- She placed his hand on the swell of her breast
- He lifted her legs over his arms
- He moved to kiss a path down her stomach
- He poised himself at her entrance
- Her nipples stabbed into his chest
- His cock betrayed him, swelling painfully
- She wrapped her legs around him, her nails digging into his shoulders as she arched into the kiss
- The strokes moved even faster against her, teasing her ectasy as she arched her back
- His hands journeyed from her hips to her waist, resting just shy of her breasts
- The moist flesh between her thighs glistening
- She gasped, grabbing fistfuls of his hair
- The first touch of his tongue between her legs made her gasp
- He licked her in long, sure strokes
- She didn't have an instant to think before he shoved her thighs wider and thrust two fingers inside her
- He claimed her breast in his hand
- Against all logic, she melted against him
- He slid his hands along her thighs until they cupped her buttocks, bringing her groin against his face
- He pulled her flush against him, feeling each soft curve melt into his chest
- He dropped a kiss between the silky valley between her breasts
- Her nipples stood up, begging for his caress
- Her nipple leapt to attention against his tongue

- He trailed his fingers down her stomach and into her wet curls
- He slid his fingers through her hot, narrow channel
- He dragged his thumb across her nub of nerves
- She arched off the mattress, whimpering, clutching his shoulders
- She cried out and dug her fingernails into his back
- Impaling herself on his stiff length with every thrust
- She could practically taste his desire
- His mouth kissed a trail to her other breast
- He drove into her, sinking deep with one strong thrust
- Her teeth nipped at his shoulder
- He leaned forward and clasped her by the waist and carefully slid her onto his thighs
- She gasped as he pressed right against the spot guaranteed to ignite her
- Her nipples beaded under his scrutiny
- The sight of her enjoying his touch was too much for him to stop
- His thumb stroked across the aching point of her nipple
- She pressed her breasts against his chest
- She arched in silent invitation
- He kissed a blazing trail down her throat
- He pulled her gown higher, until she was completely bared for his pleasure
- He stroked her bundle of nerves with his thumb
- He branded her neck with his lips, breathing fire across her skin
- His palm drifted to her thigh, lifting it around him
- She cried out as she felt him take her breast into his mouth and gently teased her nipple with his tongue
- He clasped strong arms around her, pumping up as he drew her down
- Beneath her, he bucked deeper into her and growled
- She nuzzled her face into his neck, nipping her teeth on the tendons and veins
- She held him in her hands and stroked him until he grew warm and hard
- She moved her hips gently at first, then faster
- He teased her lips with his teeth, nibbling them ever so sweetly before he nudged them apart so that he could explore every inch of her mouth with his
- She raised her hips to meet his body
- Shifting his angle to graze her pleasure spot, he filled her again
- Her legs clasped him
- Her body squeezed him tight
- He sank into her
- He drank in the intoxicating taste
- She writhed against him
- She slid her hands to his buttocks until she could cup them while he pushed himself inside her
- She could feel him pressed against hers, eager and ready
- He slid inside her, and it was tight and wet, and she could feel every inch of him working his way inside her
- With a groan, he slipped his hand from her neck down her back to her ass, leaving a trail behind his touch
- He glided a rough palm across her abdomen

- He pressed his body against the length of hers
- One hand cupped the back of her head, the other playing down the line of her body
- He put his mouth to her, ravenous for her taste
- Against his lips, she bucked, thrusting up to him
- Her sex clasped him fiercely in release
- Her nails clawed into the taut muscles encasing his shoulder blades
- He traced the outline of her bra with the tip of one finger
- He bit gently into the flesh of her breast, not hard enough to leave a mark, but just hard enough that she felt his teeth
- Her fists clasped at the sheets
- His hand stroked the upper mound of her breast
- Her spine bowed upwards as if a string pulled it
- Her chest rose and fell on ragged breaths
- That wild, predatory scent of him
- His head burrowed into the hollow of her collarbone
- He curled his fingers over the top of the towel and pushed it lower, exposing her breasts an inch at a time
- He felt her quiver in anticipation beneath his fingers
- Her sex pulsed
- His breath came harder and slow
- She parted her folds and plunged her fingers inside
- Her breathy plea went straight to his cock
- He settled his body over hers and parted her legs with his own as he settled between
- He tasted her with a slow lick
- She slid her hand up his thigh
- The feel of him brushing her legs caused things low in her stomach to clench
- The firm swell of her breasts
- Her thighs spread wide to him
- She rubbed her hand across her belly, then slid it lower, between her thighs
- He grabbed her hips and impaled her on his length in rapid-fire strokes
- She led his hand over the curve of her stomach, down to the short crisp hairs at the juncture of her thighs
- He lightly skimmed his fingers over her mons
- He reached around her to cup her breasts in his hands as he pressed himself up against her back
- He clutched her to him as he buried himself deep inside her and his body exploded in ecstasy

Emotions – Positive

- She didn't know if there was an explanation for her feelings, but she couldn't escape it
- He had the most unexplainable presence
- His usual swagger fled faster than a gambler from a bookie
- She felt her throat going dry at the enticing smell of him
- She hated how he saw right through her
- She craved the feel of his body enveloping her, driving deep
- She gazed at her watch one more time, trying to distract herself from her nagging inner thoughts
- His body burned at the memory of her touch
- Something foreign pierced his heart, some emotion he didn't even understand
- She gasped as her body erupted in chills
- Logic faded, bleeding into pure, heated need
- Orgasm soared into a sweltering bliss she'd never experienced
- The sensations swelled, congealed
- She exploded, pleasure tearing through her like nothing she'd ever felt or imagined
- As pleasure screamed inside her skin
- She removed her hands from his biceps, but the sensation of his bare skin still burned her fingers
- A warmth that might even be the stirring of deeper affection
- Something that made her feel even closer to him
- In that moment, he felt a wave of fierce protectiveness toward her
- Need roared inside him
- The entire room seemed to spin as she felt the most incredible pleasure imaginable
- Her body seemed to splinter into a thousand shards of ecstasy
- Her heart fluttered at his kindness
- It made him want to possess her, to claim her, to keep her
- Suddenly all his preparations fled his mind like scared children, his brain feeling as if it were full of static like an old television set that had lost the signal
- There was something so tender about her actions that it touched him in the strangest place
- Intense pleasure clawed up his spine
- The urge to bury himself in her slick heat pounded him
- She was warm all over, and an odd, giddy rush went through her
- Her nerve faltered at the look of him
- His head spun from the sensation
- The taste of her mouth nourished him in a way that defied description
- She bit her lip at the wave of desire those words conjured
- Delighting in the feel of her gentle touch
- The scent of her arousal drove him mad
- Her happiness woke an answering joy in him
- Anticipation for more launched through her body
- Need slammed into her
- He felt a strange sensation tighten his throat at her words

- It fired his blood to a fevered pitch
- She tried to swallow her heart back into her throat
- The need was all consuming, and yet he found the strength to keep from yielding to his lust
- His feelings confused him, and he couldn't have articulated them if he tried
- She felt her own body, beating, pulsing, living
- She was aware as never before of the workings of her flesh
- His heart was choked within his throat
- Desire tightened her nipples and flashed straight to her sex
- A thrill thrummed through her veins as she lay across his chest
- The desperate grip of his hands on her body seeped into every pore
- Her brain was clearly in her panties
- The gesture sent a wave of heat over her
- An unfamiliar tenderness swept through her
- It made her want to hug him close for being like this
- The sight of her like that set a fire inside him so hot that it was almost overwhelming
- Pleasure trickled down along every nerve ending
- Pleasure rolled through her body and she didn't fight it
- Lust crashed into him, a battering ram to the gut
- She could barely breathe around the need
- She paused as her emotions choked her
- Her skin ached to be touched
- The feel of his mouth on her was almost too intense
- He drew in a sharp breath as impatient need stabbed him and demanded he slam inside her
- She felt like Alice whisked to a surreal, but real-life Wonderland
- She felt the warmth, a surge of easiness as if returning home
- The scent of her arousal kicked up his heartbeat another notch
- Heat sizzled through her when her fingers connected with his flesh
- He kissed her neck, sending electric shivers down her spine
- A thrill of danger went through her, and she hated/cursed herself for liking it
- He became lost in her, a prisoner to the rush of electric pleasure that arced up his shaft
- Her skin jumped with a rush of lust that left her gasping
- Desire loomed, coiling
- Need stiffened his cock
- A knot of emotion burned in her centre
- A hot wash of unbridled need
- A rush of pleasure jolted her, fierce and sizzling
- The pulses of her channel pushed him to the brink
- Need ate at the chains restraining his pleasure
- Desire gathered and solidified
- She shook her head, desperately trying to think clearly despite the pleasurable sensations he was delivering
- The orgasm washed over her in a skin-shifting, nerve-dancing dance
- For a second, she felt skinless, boneless
- He wanted her as he had never had, with a frightening desperation
- He could almost hear the ticks in his heart
- He was starved for her, yet every taste did naught to assuage his hunger

- He took the kiss deeper, overwhelmed by sensation
- His dimples lowered her guard again
- Just that little touch made her tingle all over
- Passion gushed up his spine
- Pleasure pooled in his balls
- He growled at the ferocity of the pleasure that ripped through him
- The urge to release was overwhelming
- She bit her lip, trying to make her heart stop racing
- Her body responded, flowering with a tug of desire
- She let out an inward sigh of relief
- He savoured the clasp of her body and the moans he wrenched for her
- He ached to sink deep into her
- Fire and euphoria charged her veins
- With his blood surging, need pumping, breathing rough, he was losing the grip on his restraint
- Right now, as desire sizzled up his spine and emotion flooded his heart, none of it mattered
- Something in his chest twisted and roared
- Fire streaked right between her legs
- The fire grew hotter, flames licking at her self-control
- Pleasure burned her thighs
- He felt a strange stab in his middle as unfamiliar feelings washed over him
- There was a strange comfort in keeping her close to him
- Ecstasy poured across her, and there was no escape
- With every brush of his lips, his unbearably male taste saturated her senses
- He made blood rush to her face like none other, and she hated that her fair skin showed every bit of it
- She kissed him back, logical thought slipping away
- Every nerve and cell strained toward him, melted into him
- The stare he gave her sent her swam with wonder and desire
- She couldn't hide the excitement
- Her heartbeat shot to the roof
- He could feel himself being swept away by those dark eyes
- A surge of electricity ran through her veins
- He was on fire for her
- As he lunged into her again, pleasure threatened to drown him
- Between her thighs, the throbbing need nearly drowned out all else
- He was a heartbeat away from exploding
- The need to possess her utterly screamed through him
- She felt as though the world was slowly disappearing all around her
- The heat around them intensified
- She grabbed at him, clawing to keep hold of her sanity as he made her world spine away
- She took a deep breath, her heart racing
- It was insane how safe he made her feel
- She hoped the feelings were mutual, because she feared she was falling hard and fast
- Heat enveloped like a shroud
- Her heart threatened to shatter within the confines of her chest

- Desire permeated the air
- He had a smile that tugged and tingled somewhere deep and low within her belly
- His heart beating so fast/hard it felt as though it would pound its way out of his chest
- Electricity puled down her arms, bolts of hot energy that went all the way to her fingertips
- His grin sent the butterflies in her belly into a frenzy
- All the reasons to refuse scrolled through her mind
- It was a candle flame to a moth, irresistible though it burned away the wings that bore the creature to it
- Danger and desire pelted her in an unforgiving rain
- An unexpected rush of energy burst through her, like she'd been jolted with a live wire
- Desire chained him; he could not move
- The pounding in her veins refused to subside
- Her jaw tightened as a battle waged inside her – one she was afraid she could never win
- He tried to summon all the willpower he had within to keep himself in control
- He was soothing calm amidst a raging tempest
- His breath was warm against the back of her ear
- He fought the urge to draw closer to her, but lost
- In embarrassment, she looked at the ground
- The sense of attachment astounded her, like she belonged with him. To him
- For a second, she thought her heart was going to stop
- She tried to slow her heartbeat, to cool the warmth of lust that spread through her body
- Desire came knocking hard between her thighs
- Her lungs seemed to struggle to take in air
- An adrenaline rush exploded in her veins
- The sight made a field's worth of butterfly's flutter in her stomach
- Refusing to let her thoughts run away to a very dangerous place to which there was no return
- The white-hot ecstasy shimmered inside him, seeming to last forever
- She shoved that nosey little voice of reason aside
- Kicking her heartbeat into overdrive
- Heat spread through every inch of her
- Fire ran through her veins
- A flurry of sensations erupted from her belly and spread warmth between her thighs
- His touch thrilled her blood faster in his veins
- She cleared her throat and tried to ignore the feeling
- Igniting a hunger that coiled heat between her thighs
- A full-body flush tingled the tips of her ears to her toes, lingering in several places in-between
- Spiking her heartbeat into a frenzy
- Pulsing a blob between her thighs
- Air fled her lungs
- Her blood thrummed faster as she parted her lips
- Desire fevering all thoughts from his head
- The sensation travelled through her entire body, until she was more sensation than woman
- Her stomach did a little flip
- Butterflies danced in her stomach

- It felt as if she'd fallen off the precipice and into paradise
- But something about him made her insides melt
- Radiating down her spine and to her toes
- The skin prickles on the back of her neck
- Heartbeat accelerating, she …
- Adrenaline surged through her blood
- The air caught in her lungs, her pulse quickening
- Warmth flooded/bloomed in her chest
- A wild emotion washed over her, drowning her
- His tone touched her and made her ache for him
- It was so deep and intense it left her dazed and trembling
- Hearing her name on his lips sent a wave of heat from her belly to her chest
- Her heart threatened to escape her control
- Her heart hammered in her ears
- She sucked in a harsh breath and trembled with a sudden surge of heat
- Her pulse rocketed in her throat so hard she could almost taste it in the back of her throat
- His soulful dark eyes studied her with an intensity that made her skin melt
- An electric current of intense desire hit her so hard she stumbled
- The way he purred the words caused her body to tense and her lips to tingle with the urge to kiss him
- Some part of her craved him with an unreasoning madness
- He felt the heat of his desire for her all the way through his body
- She felt a strange flutter at his words and she wasn't sure why
- A weak thread of happiness pushed through her exhaustion
- Acid hatred mixed with clawing desire
- He tried to look away, but his gaze caressed her small waist, her curved hips
- He opened his eyes as a fresh rush of desire slammed him
- Want was a luxury; he needed this woman
- Fury and a flash of desire tightened his gut
- A dangerous slash of desire sliced his gut
- Her heart zoomed into hyper speed
- She flushed and tingled in some interesting places
- She tasted her pulse in her throat
- She could taste her heart thudding in her throat
- His scent, woodsy and wild, went straight to her knees
- Shards of desire needled her
- His intimate whisper sent a medley of tingles through her
-

Emotions – Negative

- Her heart sank into her belly
- Listening to him had messed up/with her head
- Her heart sank nervously
- It was stupid and probably a result of reading too many romance novels
- Shivers of panic waved like a storm
- Triggering a bittersweet knot of pain inside her
- Cold crept up her spine, fluttering like a breeze through her clothes
- Goosebumps prickle like devil's grass over her skin
- The world around her froze
- She couldn't even swallow, feeling a lump in her throat
- She did her best to suppress her inner screams
- She had too many mixed feelings orbiting in her chest
- She could feel silent anger creep up her veins
- She was shattering on the inside
- The wine-sweet taste of happiness turned sour
- She could feel reality's cold grip at her throat
- Dread slithered through her
- Foreboding bit into her belly
- Loneliness cut like a blade
- A vicious pang of jealousy pierced him
- Anger yanked hard on her, overriding sense
- Desperation clawed at her
- Desire pounded off him
- Her heart battered her ribs
- The predatory smirk in his tone sent a shiver down her spine
- A sense of foreboding settling in his stomach
- Jealous anger poured through him as he saw red over the man's words/actions
- She sank further into bleak despair
- His stomach clenched in a cold, icy knot
- The thought made her throat ache with unshed tears
- He felt a misplaced prickle of jealousy
- With a sinking heart, she watched him go
- Anger boiled in her belly
- She barely recognised him through the blur of her tears
- The realization sent another stab of pain through her heart
- She found it difficult to breathe with all the emotions that came welling up
- Her heart ached so bad she thought her chest would split wide open
- Indescribable emotions that were neither anger or despair twisted her heart
- Each word from his lips felt like a thorn digging into her heart
- She felt as if she'd stepped into a maze with no exit
- Fury boiled within her seeing him standing there so calm and collected
- Panic unfurled in her chest

- Her heart was a slow crawl in her chest
- Ice slid around his heart
- Unease stirred in his belly
- Her heart sank, and her stomach felt hollow
- The sight was an invisible fist slamming into his gut
- An icy hand curled around her heart, squeezing it tight
- A sinking feeling filled his chest
- A tiny worm of doubt began to gnaw at her
- Self-hatred threatened to choke him

Talking

- Her thoughts were interrupted by a knock on the door
- She answered with a hint of a smile on her face
- She said, wondering what she was getting herself into
- His voice sent a strange shiver to her soul
- He said, breaking the silence
- She let out a nervous laugh
- The words spilled out of her mouth spontaneously
- The words spring from her mouth
- He says from the corner of his mouth
- His tone brooks no negotiation
- The words flow without her even thinking about them
- He asked, still catching his breath
- She said over her shoulder
- He retorted testily
- She said, her eyes flashing with hope for a moment
- She said, stepping forward with a lifted chin
- Her head spun dizzily at his words
- She said, hoping her cheeks didn't betray her again
- She yelled after him playfully
- She laughed, a sound like tinkling water
- A shattered laugh escaped her lips
- His tone gave her goosebumps
- His words rang in her head
- He said, not wasting any more time
- He takes a moment to consider
- She took a moment to comprehend what he is trying to imply
- She shook her thoughts away and did her best not to succumb to his distracting comments
- He chewed on the words
- He hissed through almost-sealed lips
- He said, his voice heavy with emotion
- His voice resonates behind him
- He said with all the confidence in the world
- He forced out finally, his jaw tightening
- His words grinded like sand into her flesh
- The words force themselves out of her mouth
- She managed to ask, finally
- The cadence of her tone actually sent a shiver down his spine
- His warning tone is confident and unmistakable
- He said, his voice falling to a whisper at the final word
- Her mouth opened and shut and opened again like that of a fish suffocating in air
- No sound, save the ragged drawing of breath, emerged
- He said with deliberate slowness

- She said, hoping she sounded more confident than she felt
- She stammered, groping for words
- She swallowed hard before answering
- He said, his voice thick with possession beside her
- Amusement dripped from his voice
- His voice turns seductive and she swallow hard
- She retorted with an eye roll
- She replied, lifting her chin defiantly
- She suddenly burst out in a nervous, rapid-fire answer
- He made an exasperated sound low in his throat
- She said in what was almost a whisper
- Neither of them missed the lack of conviction in her words
- She could barely get the words past her lips
- She rasped out between sobs
- He whispered into her ear, his breath hot against her skin
- She found herself asking, even though it was a step closer to danger
- She whispered, her voice husky with emotion
- She responded, hoping her voice wouldn't break
- Although she tried to remain calm, there was a faint quiver in her voice
- His tone brokered no argument
- She was at a loss for what/how she should answer him
- He mused within her ear, his breath cascading down her neck
- He whispered in a low silky voice
- She forced out in a semi-even tone
- His words came out low, tinged with a sensual edge
- His laughter followed her outside
- She whispered with blushing cheeks
- He asked, his voice deceptively low
- She opened her mouth to speak, but words failed her
- She spoke softly, ensuring that no one else would be privy to their conversation
- The moment the words were out, she bit down on her plump bottom lip
- His words had her gaze flying to him
- His sensual voice enveloped her like black velvet
- He said, wielding a seductive smile
- His name tore from her throat, leaving it raw and brutalised
- He inquired with a quirk of his eyebrow
- She challenged, lifting a dark brow
- He breathed hard against her lips before he sampled them again
- She purred in his ear
- He blurted the sentence in one breath
- She blurted out, as insane as it sounded
- The words escaped her mouth ever so slowly
- She stressed each syllable, wishing he would understand
- His words clung to her soul
- She whispered, her eyes smouldering with lust
- He fell silent as he realised the truth

Facial Descriptions

- His eyes glittered
- His eyes scanned her in the most unusual way
- A soft smirk of mischief softened by the dimples in both cheeks
- A strand of black hair dangled on his forehead
- His eyes are unusually piercing
- She could see the veins pumping on his neck
- There is an indecipherable look in his eyes
- He turned his head toward her and smiled
- Her eyes were like a clear blue ocean on a sunny day
- She flushed
- She saw the shock register on my face before I could hide it
- A thin, almost unnoticeable hint of a smile curved on his lips
- A single sticky tear rolled down her cheek
- The regret in his eyes was unmistakable
- A faint smile lined her lips
- His head cocked to the side, his eyes shifting from the ground to her
- He tongued his cheek from the inside
- Her lips were dry
- His eyes scanned her thoroughly
- A seductive gleam flowering in his eyes
- A huge smirk invaded his face
- She craned her neck, looking at him with surprise in her eyes
- He nods with closed eyes
- He turned with a blazing fire burning in his eyes
- He kept nodding, a smile creasing his lips
- Blue eyes observed his approach
- She had to concentrate, push aside all expression from her face, and play the game
- She paused and licked her lips
- Surprise twisting his features
- His eyes alight with anticipation
- Her dark eyes dancing with passion
- His black brows winged down
- A million questions stormed through her eyes
- She bit her lip hard around the smile that tugged at her mouth
- Dimples adorning his cheeks
- A rush of colour crept up his neck, tinting him pink
- Her cheeks were stained pink
- Heat rushed up her face
- His long hair flew in tangles across his face
- His eyes locked onto hers with an intensity she couldn't escape
- The teeth of his smile shone white
- His eyes were fathomless, an abyss that promised nothing but desire and endless bliss

- His eyes were demanding and passionate, hungry for something she herself was starving for
- She shook her head, not knowing how to articulate to him what was going through her mind
- He tilted his head to the side, a smirk forming on his face
- He had a triumphant smirk on his face as he eyed her from head to foot
- Her face turned serious and she creased her brows
- When she glanced back, she could see him looking at her with a strange expression on his face
- She felt the heat climb up her face and knew she was blushing
- He stared at her, as if trying to gauge her reaction
- A fierce heat burned in his eyes as he curled his lips into a smile
- His pupils the colour and sheen of polished obsidian
- He regarded her steadily with his green eyes and she found she couldn't look away
- He looked straight at her, undaunted, and smiled guilelessly
- A self-satisfied smile appeared on his face
- He fixed his eyes on her, those eyes that seemed as though they could see every thought and feeling that ran through her mind/head
- His eyes met hers, his gaze so deep, so intensive that her whole body shuddered
- She saw his expression change to something fierce and dangerous
- Embarrassment reddened her cheeks
- His head tilted down as his eyes bored into hers, causing shadows to cascade beneath his sharp cheekbones
- A mischievous grin pinned to her mouth
- She zeroed in on his perfectly formed full lips and his dark, intelligent eyes
- A sheepish twitch curled the corner of his mouth
- A sceptical frown pulled at his mouth
- She said on a laugh
- He gazed at her with his eyebrows lifted, a one-sided smile tilting his lips
- She lifted an eyebrow, trying unsuccessfully to trap her smile before it blossomed over her face
- She bit the inside of her cheek
- He cocked his head to one side
- Energy rippled between their locked gazes
- His gaze lingered on her lips, sparking a blazing fire in his eyes
- His gaze was a warm caress
- A lopsided grin adorned his full lips
- Heat spread through her cheeks
- The right corner of his mouth upturned into a half grin
- Her eyes were encased in the longest lashes he had ever seen
- His eyelashes lowered, shielding his eyes from her
- A burst of heat lashed at her face
- Her lips were upturned into a graceful smile
- That smile of his turned almost dangerously sexy
- She turned her eyes on him and he was taken by their colour, blue as the sky
- Her smile coaxed him to touch her, to challenge him to walk away
- His mouth twisted in a mysterious smile, as if he knew he made her nervous
- Those pale eyes, framed by thick black lashes, drew her without mercy

- His mouth sharpened into a dangerous slash
- He flashed his signature grin
- His eyes glowed hot with lust
- There was a dark light in his eyes, something more primitive than mere words could describe
- His laser-focused gaze burned her lips, her body
- He stared at the hunger in her brilliant gaze
- She saw something inside him unleash
- Desire leapt in her vivid eyes
- He cut a hungry glance in her direction
- When their stares met, his mouth lifted in a wicked smile
- His eyes glittered as they locked with hers
- He gave her a charming grin at that, but she didn't buy it
- His lips curved up on one side in a wry smile
- His flirting eyes were all over her already
- He stared with interest
- Her expression alight with anticipation
- His eyes were thrown into shadow
- She pressed her lips together to hold in a smile
- The smile that broke out across her face blinded him with its beauty
- Cunning swirled in his eyes
- There was no missing the disappointment in her gaze
- There was something so sexy in that vulnerable look of his
- Those dark eyes singed her

Sounds

- The sound of the door closing behind her echoed in the back of her head
- Her laugh echoed behind the door she slammed
- Thunder cracked overhead as the sky grew cloudy
- Silence stole her breath away
- The only sounds that could be heard were the thin whistle of the wind through the trees and the distant cry of an owl
- Her breathing sawed in and out
- A growl started low in his chest, climbing up his throat to spill out in a snarl from his lips
- A low growl trickled from his lips
- A low sound came from deep in his throat
- A deep chuckle resonated through the phone
- Insects buzzed just above the surface of the water
- A loud, calling whistle blasted through the trees
- A growl resounds in her ear
- Birds scattered from the surrounding trees, flying blindly into the sky
- She listened to the sound of the raindrops
- A whimper slid from her lips
- Her moan was pleasure-filled
- The sea crashed against the rock as though it were trying to seize them
- That noise filtered through the trees again
- A sharp rap against the cottage's front window startled him
- A faint crunch of footsteps
- The door chime signalling her departure sounded loudly in the room's silence
- The door chime sounded, startling them
- The chime sounded, drowned out by the door crashing against the wall
- A sensual ballad drifted through the speakers
- The voice sounded far away, but he knew it and held onto it
- His chair creaked against the floor
- The sound of dripping water receded
- Excited voices bounced off the rock walls
- A melodic sound, like the pealing of silver bells
- The sounds of branches groaning in the wind
- Footsteps behind her played around the edges of her hearing
- A guttural sound came deep from within his throat
- She let herself soak in the ambient music for a few moments, wondering what the words were and drinking in the fragranced air
- She was lost under the saxophone notes that jumped and danced in the smoky cavern
- A buzz of excited talk

Romantic Settings

- A castle/mansion
- Beside a waterfall
- An open-top bus
- In the rain at night
- A picnic in the park
- In the forest
- On the beach
- A vineyard
- A quiet little bistro/café
- The stairs covered in rose petals, tealight candles on each step
- Under a tree
- The bath-tub
- A hotel
- A table overlooking the water (sea, lake, pond)
- A narrow alley with fairy-lights strung overhead
- Walking by the riverfront
- A music festival
- A museum
- A sleigh ride
- A log cabin in the wilderness
- A horse-back ride
- In the mountains
- A hot spring resort
- An art gallery
- An old church or temple
- Beside a log fire
- A BBQ
- A gondola/canal ride
- A rowboat/yacht
- A jazz club
- A pagoda/bandstand
- A wedding
- A holiday/vacation
- An aeroplane
- A train
- An ice rink in the middle of a busy city
- Under the cherry blossoms
- A rose garden
- A deserted island
- A helicopter ride
- Ancient ruins

- A quaint British pub
- A cottage near a cliff

Words Used in Sex Scenes

- Settled over
- Positioned over
- Glided into/over
- Rocked against
- Bobbed
- Bear down on
- Lifted
- Entwined
- Spread
- Pinned
- Grind
- Covered
- Guided
- Rotated
- Twisted
- Encircled
- Tweaked
- Nestled
- Surrounded
- Bared
- Straddled
- Caressed
- Soothed
- Massaged
- Worshiped
- Lathed
- Trailed
- Swiped
- Journeyed
- Take
- Swirled
- Tugged
- Yanked
- Rolled
- Brushed
- Swept
- Finger
- Sear
- Kneaded
- Clasped
- Grasped
- Stroked

- Scorched
- Held down
- Impaled
- Seized
- Ravished
- Wriggled
- Clung
- Nuzzled
- Clutched
- Possessed
- Scraped
- Plunged
- Pushed
- Ravaged
- Burrowed
- Breached
- Pierced
- Licked
- Sucked
- Bit
- Nibbled

Words for Genitalia

- Penis
- Cock
- Dick
- Junk
- Staff
- Meat
- Pole
- Bulge
- Cockhead
- Length
- Organ
- Ridge
- Crown
- Corona
- Erection
- Phallus
- Privates
- Flesh
- Foreskin
- Hard-on
- Head
- Johnson
- Wang
- Schlong
- Balls
- Groin
- Gonads
- Testicles
- Nuts
- Jewels
- Stones
- Testes
- Scrotum
- Nipples
- Crotch
- Clitoris
- Clitty
- Gem
- Hood
- Love button
- Nub

- Nubbin
- Tissue
- Pleasure spot
- Nerve centre
- Clit
- Bud
- Bundle of nerves
- Vagina
- Area
- Canal
- Womanhood
- Wetness
- Sheath
- Slit
- Cunny
- Crease
- Cleft
- Heat
- Honey-pot
- Mons
- vulva
- Cunt
- Pussy
- Lips
- Labia
- Cervix
- Womb
- Uterus
- G-spot
- Sweet spot
- Pubes
- Pubic hair
- Soft curls
- Sex
- Secret place
- Hymen
- Breast
- Tit
- Boob
- Funbags
- Bosom
- Chest
- Cleavage
- Hooters
- Jugs
- Mounds

- Melons
- Rack
- Tatas
- Orbs
- Pillows
- Bust

Conclusion

Writing romance can be just as exciting as experiencing it. Whether it is clean, comedy, erotic, interracial, sci-fi, contemporary, medical, holiday/vacation, paranormal, or any other sub-genre of romance, these books have the ability to steal readers' breath and swoon over the characters.

Sometimes, however, writing it can be a little difficult, especially when you're trying not to repeat the same descriptions over and over again. *The Writer's Guidebook to Writing Love, Romance, and Sex Scenes,* along with my other books in the series, was designed to help other writers as they create their own novels and take some of that pressure off.

It is my hope that this book will help you complete your novel and inspire readers all around the world with your words.

Happy writing!

Author's Note

If you enjoyed this book or found it helpful, please consider writing a review on Amazon. It doesn't have to be much, a simple 'I liked it,' is enough. You can also find more of my books that may be helpful when writing your novel.

1000 Plot Twists for Your Next Novel

THE WRITER'S GUIDEBOOK

TO FACIAL DESCRIPTIONS
AND BODY LANGUAGE

S L LETHE

THE WRITER'S GUIDEBOOK

TO WRITING

FIGHT SCENES

S L LETHE

Printed in Poland
by Amazon Fulfillment
Poland Sp. z o.o., Wrocław

61717420R00027